GIGANTOPITHECUS SIMPLIFIED

GIGANTOPITHECUS SIMPLIFIED

SOLOMON HATHAWAY

Revitalized Occult and Strange

Published by Revitalized Occult and Strange, an imprint
of Bald and Bonkers Network LLC.

CONTENTS

CHAPTER 1

Introduction

The colossal Gigantopithecus roamed southern China from around 2 million to 300,000 years ago, in the Early to Middle Pleistocene era. This giant ape is known through fossilized remains—primarily teeth and jawbones—unearthed across China, Thailand, Vietnam, and Indonesia. The initial find, a pair of large teeth, emerged in 1935 in a drugstore, discovered by the anthropologist Ralph von Koenigswald. Subsequent discoveries have included over a thousand teeth and several jawbones scattered across various sites.

Initially believed to be a human ancestor,

Gigantopithecus is now considered closer to orangutans. Estimates suggest it was an enormous creature, weighing in at 440 to 660 pounds, although the exact size is hard to pin down due to the limited remains. There seemed to be significant size variation between males and females. The ape's dentition was distinctive, featuring large molars designed for grinding down tough, fibrous vegetation. Its tooth enamel was remarkably thick, an adaptation for consuming coarse foods like stems and roots.

As a generalist herbivore, Gigantopithecus fed on a diverse array of forest plants. It thrived in subtropical to tropical climates but vanished around 300,000 years ago, possibly due to climatic shifts impacting its environment or interactions with early humans. In modern times, Gigantopithecus has been romantically linked to legendary beings such as the Tibetan yeti and the American bigfoot, figures woven into local lore and the subject of cryptozoological study.

CHAPTER 2

Discovery

In 1935, the anthropologist Ralph von Koenigswald named the species Gigantopithecus blacki upon the discovery of two exceptionally large lower molar teeth, each measuring 20 mm by 22 mm. These teeth were found in a Hong Kong apothecary, sold as "dragon bones" used in traditional Chinese medicine. The species was named in honor of Davidson Black, a Canadian paleoanthropologist who had recently died and had contributed significantly to the study of human evolution in China.

While working for the Dutch East Indies Mineralogical Survey in Indonesia, von Koenigswald continued to discover more teeth and concluded that they probably originated from the Guangdong or Guangxi regions of China. World War II, however, interrupted his work, as he was interned by Japanese forces, delaying the official description of the type specimen until 1952. The initial teeth von Koenigswald found now reside in the collection of the University of Utrecht.

In 1955, under the direction of Chinese paleontologist Pei Wenzhong and the Chinese Institute of Vertebrate Paleontology and Paleoanthropology, a discovery of 47 teeth was made in Guangdong and Guangxi, mingled with shipments labeled "dragon bones." The following year, the first on-site Gigantopithecus remains, a third molar and a premolar, were uncovered in a cave on Niusui Mountain, Guangxi, aptly named "Gigantopithecus Cave." In the same year, Xiuhuai Qin, a farmer from Liucheng, stumbled upon more teeth and the first mandible in his field. Subsequent years saw the team excavate more mandibles and over a thousand teeth in the area.

Gigantopithecus fossils have been unearthed at 16 different locations throughout southern China, stretching from Longgupo and Longgudong in the north to Hainan Island in the south. Isolated finds in Vietnam and Thailand might also be attributed to Gigantopithecus, though they could represent another extinct orangutan species. The oldest of these remains are dated to 2 million years ago, with the most recent being between 380,000 and 310,000 years old. The prevalence of teeth over other bones is largely due to porcupines, which chew on bones for nutrients and tend to store them in caves, often leaving teeth intact because of their durable enamel. This peculiar behavior accounts for the abundance of teeth compared to other skeletal remains.

CHAPTER 3

Classification

Gigantopithecus, known scientifically as G. blacki, was initially thought by researchers like von Koenigswald in 1935 to be related to ancient apes like Sivapithecus from India. Later, in 1939, Robert Broom suggested it might be closely related to Australopithecus, an early human ancestor. Franz Weidenreich in 1946 even speculated it could be a giant human ancestor, calling it "Gigantanthropus." This idea was part of a theory proposing that different human races evolved independently from local ancient human species.

By 1952, von Koenigswald agreed that

Gigantopithecus belonged to the human family tree, but not directly as an ancestor. Over the years, there was much debate about whether Gigantopithecus was a human ancestor until the Out of Africa theory became widely accepted, suggesting human origins in Africa rather than Asia.

Today, Gigantopithecus is classified within the same group as orangutans, known as Ponginae. However, similarities between Gigantopithecus and orangutans are scarce due to incomplete fossil evidence. Some researchers in 2017 proposed that Gigantopithecus might be more closely related to Lufengpithecus from China, which lived millions of years earlier.

Recent studies in 2019 used protein analysis from a Gigantopithecus tooth to confirm its close relationship with orangutans. It's estimated that Gigantopithecus and orangutans shared a common ancestor about 12 to 10 million years ago during the Miocene period, a time when many ape species were evolving. This research also suggests that the Ponginae lineage split from African great apes around 26 to 17.7 million years ago.

A jawbone unearthed in 1969, estimated to be 8.6 million years old, was discovered in the Sivalik Hills in northern India. It was named "G. bilaspurensis" by paleontologists Elwyn L. Simons and Shiv Raj Kumar Chopra, who speculated it could be an ancestor of G. blacki. This find was similar to a molar discovered in 1915 on Pakistan's Pothohar Plateau, originally termed "Dryopithecus giganteus." Later, Von Koenigswald reclassified it as Indopithecus in 1950. However, it was renamed "G. giganteus" by American anthropologists Frederick Szalay and Eric Delson in 1979, a name that remained until 2003 when Australian anthropologist David W. Cameron reverted it to Indopithecus. Presently, "G. bilaspurensis" is recognized as the same species as Indopithecus giganteus, which consolidates Gigantopithecus into a single recognized species, G. blacki.

CHAPTER 4

Description

Size

Determining the full size of Gigantopithecus is a complex task, as only dental and mandibular remains are available for study. Not all ancient primates with large teeth and thick enamel were necessarily of great size. Weidenreich proposed in 1946 that Gigantopithecus might have been double the size of an adult male gorilla. By 1957, Pei's estimates suggested a height of around 12 feet. In 1970, Simons and Ettel posited a near 9-foot stature and a weight up to 600 pounds, roughly 40% greater than that of a standard male gorilla. Johnson, in 1979, extrapolated from gorilla dimensions to conjecture that Gigantopithecus's femur and humerus were approximately 20–25% longer than those of gorillas. More recently, in 2017, Zhang and Harrison offered a weight range of 440 to 660 pounds for the creature. However, without more comprehensive fossil records, these figures remain speculative.

Sexual Dimorphism

Gigantopithecus exhibited clear sexual dimorphism, with males being significantly larger than females. The size difference is evident in their dental dimensions; male upper canines averaged 0.83 inches in length compared to the 0.61 inches of their female counterparts. Furthermore, Mandible III, presumed to belong to a male, was 40% larger than Mandible I, associated with a female. Such disparity in size between the sexes is seen to a greater extent only in gorillas among contemporary apes, especially regarding canine size, and remains unparalleled in jaw size variation.

Teeth and Jaws

Gigantopithecus shared a common dental formula with other apes, featuring two incisors, one canine, two premolars, and three molars on each side of both jaws. The canines were robust, without the typical sharpening traits, indicating a role similar to that of premolars and molars. Notably smaller incisors and wear patterns on their lingual aspect hinted at an underbite. Chewing involved a side-to-side jaw motion, and the tooth roots were notably elongated relative to the crown. Among apes, its molars were exceptionally large, with the biggest ones in the lower jaw reaching dimensions of 0.80 by 0.82 inches. The molar enamel was the thickest seen in any ape, measuring up to 0.24 inches on the side facing the tongue, reminiscent of the extinct Paranthropus. These molars had flat surfaces for grinding and were quite tall, with the enamel rising above the level of the gums.

CHAPTER 5

Palaeobiology

Diet

Gigantopithecus mainly ate plants. Studies using carbon-13 isotopes suggest it favored C3 plants like fruits, leaves, and other forest plants. Its strong jaw was capable of handling tough or hard foods, even though its dental anatomy, similar to modern apes that eat soft leaves or seeds, suggests it may have had a varied diet like chimpanzees. Unlike orangutans, Gigantopithecus had teeth with fewer marks from eating small, hard objects, indicating it likely had a broad diet.

Its teeth, with molar-like premolars and large

molars with long roots, suggest it crushed and ground bulky, fibrous foods. The thick enamel on its teeth, which is the hardest part, suggests it could handle abrasive foods like dirt particles found on plants near the ground, such as bamboo shoots. Analysis also suggests it ate stems, roots, and grasses, but not the grasses found on savannas. In one cave, evidence suggests it ate fruits like figs and mulberries.

As its environment changed over time, especially near its extinction about 400,000 to 320,000 years ago, Gigantopithecus in southeastern China may have adapted to new food sources. Teeth from this period show different features, possibly reflecting this adaptation.

Gigantopithecus was once thought to be a predator that lived in caves, but its teeth and jaw structure clearly show it was adapted for plant-eating. Some researchers compared its teeth to those of giant pandas, suggesting they may have filled a similar ecological niche as bamboo specialists, although Gigantopithecus had thicker enamel and different tooth shapes.

Unfortunately, its reliance on specific types of bark and twigs for food might have contributed to its eventual extinction.

Growth

Gigantopithecus took a long time to develop its third molar. It required about 600-800 days for the enamel on the cusps to form, which is quite lengthy. Overall, the entire molar took approximately four years to fully form. This timeframe is similar to what is observed in humans and chimpanzees. Enamel formation near the enamel-dentine junction began at a rate of about four micrometers per day, a rate seen in baby teeth of modern apes.

Pathology

Gigantopithecus had a high rate of cavities in its molars, estimated at 11%. This suggests that fruit might have been a common part of its diet. Molars from Gigantopithecus Cave often show pitting enamel hypoplasia, where the enamel forms improperly with pits and grooves. This condition can result from malnutrition during growth years, indicating periods of food scarcity. It can also be caused by other factors. For example, specimen PA1601-1 from Yanliang Cave shows evidence of losing the right second molar before the neighboring third molar erupted, suggesting this individual managed to survive despite difficulties with chewing.

Society

Gigantopithecus displayed high levels of sexual dimorphism, suggesting intense competition among males. However, unlike modern non-human apes where displaying upper canines is important in aggressive behavior, this feature was less significant for Gigantopithecus.

CHAPTER 6

Palaeoecology

Gigantopithecus fossils are mostly found in South China, where there were subtropical evergreen forests. Hainan, however, had a tropical rainforest. Studies of Gigantopithecus teeth from the Early Pleistocene suggest they lived in dense, humid forests with closed canopies. For example, Queque Cave had a mix of deciduous and evergreen trees like birch, oak, and chinkapin, along with low-lying plants like herbs and ferns.

The "Gigantopithecus fauna" is a significant group of mammals from the Early Pleistocene in southern China. It spans three periods: 2.6–1.8

million years ago, 1.8–1.2 million years ago, and 1.2–0.8 million years ago. In the early period, it included ancient animals like Sinomastodon (related to elephants), Hesperotherium (a chalicothere), Hippopotamodon (a suid), Dorcabune (a tragulid), and Cervavitus (a deer). The middle period saw the arrival of Ailuropoda wulingshanensis (a panda), Cuon antiquus (a dhole), and Tapirus sinensis (a tapir). The late period featured animals like Ailuropoda baconi (another panda) and Stegodon (a stegodontid proboscidean).

The Gigantopithecus fauna also included orangutans, macaques, rhinos, extinct pigs like Sus xiaozhu and Sus peii, muntjac (a type of deer), gaur (a type of cow), Megalovis (a bovid), and occasionally large saber-toothed cats like Megantereon. In 2009, Russel Ciochon suggested a chimp-sized ape, identified later as Meganthropus, lived alongside Gigantopithecus. Longgudong Cave possibly bridged the gap between the Palaearctic and Oriental regions, housing both typical Gigantopithecus fauna and animals from colder climates like hedgehogs, hyenas, horses, Leptobos (a bovid), and pikas.

CHAPTER 7

Extinction

During the Pleistocene, Gigantopithecus adapted to its environment, exhibiting dietary shifts in response to ecological stress, as evidenced by its dental morphology. In contrast, other contemporary hominids displayed less pronounced changes.

The late Middle Pleistocene to early Middle Pleistocene was marked by intense glacial cycles, shifts towards colder or wetter conditions, more pronounced seasonal variations, and a decline in C4 vegetation. The dynamics of winter and summer monsoons were also influential during this period in China.

Stratigraphic data indicates that Gigantopithecus's habitat range contracted from the Guangxi, Guizhou, and Hainan provinces to solely Guangxi between 420,000 and 330,000 years ago. By 300,000 years ago, this giant ape's population dwindled further as its forest habitats gave way to expanding grasslands. It is estimated that Gigantopithecus became extinct between 295,000 and 215,000 years ago, a timeline that aligns with heightened seasonality and significant environmental shifts.

The extinction of Gigantopithecus, which was specialized in its environment, contrasts with the survival of Pongo weidenreichi (a type of orangutan) and Homo (human ancestors) in the Middle Pleistocene. Pongo weidenreichi likely had more flexible eating habits across seasons, while Homo was adaptable to various habitats due to its generalist diet. Some researchers suggested that Homo erectus may have contributed to the extinction of Gigantopithecus, although human activity in southern China wasn't prevalent until after

Gigantopithecus disappeared. It remains uncertain whether competition for resources or hunting by early humans were factors in its extinction.

There are suggestions by some researchers that Gigantopithecus might have survived into the early Late Pleistocene, but evidence supporting this is limited.

CHAPTER 8

Cryptozoology

In the realm of cryptozoology, Gigantopithecus is often associated with legendary creatures such as the Tibetan Yeti and the American Bigfoot, both of which are depicted as apelike giants in local folklore. The link was first suggested in 1960 by zoologist Wladimir Tschernezky, who referenced a photograph of supposed Yeti tracks from 1951 in the journal Nature, proposing that the Yeti's bipedal gait and appearance might be similar to that of Gigantopithecus. This hypothesis garnered initial scientific curiosity, leading to further discussions in prominent journals like Nature and Science, and also ignited widespread public intrigue, fueling ongoing quests to find these elusive beings.

Anthropologist Grover Krantz was a prominent figure in this field, actively pursuing evidence for the existence of these cryptids from 1970 until his passing in 2002. He postulated that Bigfoot could be a descendant of Gigantopithecus, even suggesting the name "Gigantopithecus canadensis" for the North American variant. Despite his dedication, Krantz's theories were met with skepticism and criticism from both the scientific community and enthusiasts, due to his acceptance of evidence that many deemed unreliable.

CHAPTER 9

References

1. von Koenigswald, G. H. R. (1935). "Eine fossile Säugetierfauna mit Simia aus Südchina" (PDF). *Proceedings of the Koninklijke Akademie van Wetenschappen te Amsterdam*. 38 (8): 874–879. Archived (PDF) from the original on 2017-12-12. Retrieved 2017-12-12.
2. "Definition of gigantopithecus | Dictionary.com". www.dictionary.com. Archived from the original on 2022-10-03. Retrieved 2022-10-02.

3. Tamisiea, Jack (10 January 2024). "The Biggest Ape That Ever Lived Was Not Too Big to Fail - Fossil teeth reveal Gigantopithecus was doomed by a changing environment and an inflexible diet". *The New York Times*. Archived from the original on 10 January 2024. Retrieved 11 January 2024.

4. Zhang, Yingqi; Westaway, Kira E.; Haberle, Simon; et al. (10 January 2024). "The demise of the giant ape Gigantopithecus blacki". *Nature*. 625 (7995): 535–539. doi:10.1038/s41586-023-06900-0. PMC 10794149. PMID 38200315.

5. Zhang, Y.; Harrison, T. (2017). "Gigantopithecus blacki: a giant ape from the Pleistocene of Asia revisited". *American Journal of Physical Anthropology*. 162 (S63): 153–177. doi:10.1002/ajpa.23150. PMID 28105715.

6. Hartwig, W. C. (2002). *The Primate Fossil Record*. Cambridge University Press. pp. 371–372. ISBN 978-0-521-66315-1.

7. Poirier, F.E.; McKee, J.K. (1999). *Understanding Human Evolution* (fourth ed.).

Upper Saddle River, New Jersey: Prentice Hall. p. 119. ISBN 0-13-096152-3.

8. Coichon, R. (1991). "The ape that was – Asian fossils reveal humanity's giant cousin". *Natural History*. 100: 54–62. ISSN 0028-0712. Archived from the original on May 25, 2015.

9. Sofwan, N.; et al. (2016). "Primata Besar di Jawa: Spesimen Baru Gigantopithecus dari Semedo" [Giant Primate of Java: A new Gigantopithecus specimen from Semedo]. *Berkala Arkeologi*. 36 (2): 141–160. doi:10.30883/jba.v36i2.241.

10. Zhang, Y.; Jin, C.; et al. (2015). "A fourth mandible and associated dental remains of Gigantopithecus blacki from the Early Pleistocene Yanliang Cave, Fusui, Guangxi, South China". *Historical Biology*. 28 (1–2): 95–104. doi:10.1080/08912963.2015.1024115.   S2CID 130928802.

11. Broom, R. (1939). "The dentition of the Transvaal Pleistocene anthropoids, Plesianthropus and Paranthropus" (PDF).

Annals of the Transvaal Museum. 19 (3): 303–314.

12. Weidenreich, F. (1946). *Apes, Giants, and Man*. University of Chicago Press. pp. 58–66.

13. von Koenigswald, G. H. R. (1952). "Gigantopithecus blacki von Koenigswald, a giant fossil hominoid from the Pleistocene of southern China". *Anthropological Papers of the American Museum of Natural History*. 43: 292–325. hdl:2246/298.

14. Welker, F.; Ramos-Madrigal, J.; Kuhlwilm, M.; et al. (2019). "Enamel proteome shows that Gigantopithecus was an early diverging pongine". *Nature*. 576 (7786): 262–265. doi:10.1038/s41586-019-1728-8. PMC 6908745. PMID 31723270.

15. Szalay, F.; Delson, E. (1979). *Evolutionary History of the Primates*. Academic Press. pp. 493–494. ISBN 978-1-4832-8925-0.

16. Cameron, D. (2003). "A functional and phylogenetic interpretation of the late Miocene Siwalik hominid Indopithecus and the Chinese Pleistocene hominid Gigantopithecus". *Himalayan Geology*. 24: 19–28.

17. Cameron, D. (2001). "The taxonomic status of the Siwalik late Miocene hominid Indopithecus (= Gigantopithecus)". *Himalayan Geology*. 22: 29–34.

18. Olejniczak, A. J.; et al. (2008). "Molar enamel thickness and dentine horn height in Gigantopithecus blacki" (PDF). *American Journal of Physical Anthropology*. 135 (1): 85–91. doi:10.1002/ajpa.20711. PMID 17941103. Archived from the original (PDF) on 2016-03-03.

19. Johnson, A. E. Jr. (1979). "Skeletal Estimates of Gigantopithecus Based on a Gorilla Analogy". *Journal of Human Evolution*. 8 (6): 585–587. doi:10.1016/0047-2484(79)90111-8.

20. Dean, M. C.; Schrenk, F. (2003). "Enamel thickness and development in a third permanent molar of Gigantopithecus blacki". *Journal of Human Evolution*. 45 (5): 381–388. doi:10.1016/j.jhevol.2003.08.009. PMID 14624748.

21. Ciochon, R.; et al. (1996). "Dated Co-Occurrence of Homo erectus and Gigantopithecus from Tham Khuyen Cave,

Vietnam". *Proceedings of the National Academy of Sciences of the United States of America*. 93 (7): 3016–3020. doi:10.1073/pnas.93.7.3016. PMC 39753. PMID 8610161.

22. Kono, R. T.; Zhang, Y.; Jin, C.; Takai, M.; Suwa, G. (2014). "A 3-dimensional assessment of molar enamel thickness and distribution pattern in Gigantopithecus blacki". *Quaternary International*. 354: 46–51. doi:10.1016/j.quaint.2014.02.012.

23. Shao, q.; Wang, Y.; et al. (2017). "U-series and ESR/U-series dating of the Stegodon–Ailuropoda fauna at Black Cave, Guangxi, southern China with implications for the timing of the extinction of Gigantopithecus blacki". *Quaternary International*. 434: 65–74. doi:10.1016/j.quaint.2015.12.016.

24. Bocherens, H.; Schrenk, F.; Chaimanee, Y.; et al. (2017). "Flexibility of diet and habitat in Pleistocene South Asian mammals: Implications for the fate of the giant fossil ape Gigantopithecus". *Quaternary International*. 434: 148–155. doi:10.1016/j.quaint.2015.11.059.

25. Kupczik, K.; Dean, M. C. (2008). "Comparative observations on the tooth root morphology of Gigantopithecus blacki". *Journal of Human Evolution*. 54 (2): 196–204. doi:10.1016/j.jhevol.2007.09.013. PMID 18045651.

26. Ciochon, R.; Piperno, D. R.; Thompson, R. G. (1990). "Opal phytoliths found on the teeth of the extinct ape Gigantopithecus blacki: implications for paleodietary studies". *Proceedings of the National Academy of Sciences*. 87 (20): 8120–8124. doi:10.1073/pnas.87.20.8120. PMC 54904. PMID 2236026.

27. Qu, Y.; Jin, C.; Zhang, Y.; et al. (2014). "Preservation assessments and carbon and oxygen isotopes analysis of tooth enamel of Gigantopithecus blacki and contemporary animals from Sanhe Cave, Chongzuo, South China during the Early Pleistocene".

28. Zanolli, Clément; Kullmer, Ottmar; Kelley, Jay; Bacon, Anne-Marie; Demeter, Fabrice; Dumoncel, Jean; Fiorenza, Luca; Grine, Frederick E.; Hublin, Jean-Jacques; Nguyen, Anh Tuan; Nguyen, Thi Mai Huong (May

2019). "Evidence for increased hominid diversity in the Early to Middle Pleistocene of Indonesia" (PDF). Nature Ecology & Evolution. 3 (5): 755–764. doi:10.1038/s41559-019-0860-z. PMID 30962558. S2CID 102353734. Retrieved 2022-11-17.

29. Sun, Fajun; Wang, Yang; Wang, Yuan; Jin, Chang-zhu; Deng, Tao; Wolff, Burt (15 June 2019). "Paleoecology of Pleistocene mammals and paleoclimatic change in South China: Evidence from stable carbon and oxygen isotopes". Palaeogeography, Palaeoclimatology, Palaeoecology. 524: 1–12. doi:10.1016/j.palaeo.2019.03.021. S2CID 134558136. Archived from the original on 14 November 2022. Retrieved 14 November 2022.

30. Louys, J.; Roberts, P. (2020). "Environmental Drivers of Megafauna and Hominin Extinction in South East Asia". Nature. 586 (7829): 402–406. doi:10.1038/s41586-020-2810-y. hdl:10072/402368. PMID 33029012. S2CID 222217295.

31. Zhao, L.X.; Zhang, L.Z. (12 February 2013).

"New fossil evidence and diet analysis of Gigantopithecus blacki and its distribution and extinction in South China". Quaternary International. 286: 69–74. doi:10.1016/j.quaint.2011.12.016. ISSN 1040-6182.

32. Lopatin, A. V.; Maschenko, E. N.; Dac, Le Xuan (June 2022). "Gigantopithecus blacki (Primates, Ponginae) from the Lang Trang Cave (Northern Vietnam): The Latest Gigantopithecus in the Late Pleistocene?". Doklady Biological Sciences. 502 (1): 6–10. doi:10.1134/S0012496622010069. ISSN 0012-4966. PMID 35298746. S2CID 254413457.

33. Regal, B. (2008). "Amateur versus professional: the search for Bigfoot". Endeavour. 32 (2): 53–57. doi:10.1016/j.endeavour.2008.04.005. PMID 18514914.